HOME BUYER'S GUIDE

*H*ome.

Where you and your family live and laugh together...where you enjoy today and plan for tomorrow.

Buying a home is still as much a part of the American Dream as ever. It is one of the biggest decisions you will make, not one to be taken lightly. Homes cost a lot of money and require a commitment to maintenance. Renting is much less complicated. So why buy a home?

Home ownership provides key financial benefits. Owning your own home gives you a sense of freedom, a feeling of security and pride. All in all, home ownership is generally a high-performing investment well worth the effort.

Now that you've decided to investigate home ownership, the best way to approach your purchase is as an educated consumer. Take the time to read this booklet thoroughly and review the benefits in detail. Completing the worksheets will help you make the final decision. Make note of your questions and concerns as you read. Your CENTURY 21® sales professional will be able to help you with the answers.

Nearly a million families a year become homeowners for the first time. You can be one of them.

THE BENEFITS

FINANCIAL BENEFITS

Through home ownership, the money you pay for shelter every month will be an investment in your future, not someone else's. Each mortgage check you write will build equity—the difference between what your home is worth now and what you paid for it. When you sell, you collect the equity as your profit. This profit can help put you into your next, larger home. Or you can tap the equity for college tuition loans or retirement funds at a rate which is generally lower than available on personal loans. Also, paying on and ultimately paying off a mortgage is an excellent way to establish a good credit rating and prove financial stability.

Equity	Current Dollars	Inflation-adjusted Dollars
After 5 years	$ 43,000	$36,000
After 10 years	$ 80,000	$54,000
After 15 years	$127,000	$71,000

To see how quickly equity can build, suppose you purchase a home for $100,000. After a 25 percent down payment of $25,000, you are left with a $75,000 mortgage. On a 30-year conventional loan with an interest rate of 10.5 percent, your monthly payments (principal and interest only, not including taxes and insurance) would be $686. With a hypothetical appreciation rate of five percent per year and transfer costs of nine percent at the time you sell the house, you would realize equity at the rate shown.

Your home purchase is not only an investment in your future, it's a powerful tax benefit as well. You can deduct both the interest on home mortgage payments as well as the cost of property taxes.

PERSONAL FREEDOM

Home ownership frees you from the whims and dictates of a landlord. There will be no unexpected rent hikes. You will be able to decorate as you like, have a dog or cat, and make improvements on your property. You gain privacy and the freedom of expression.

PRIDE OF OWNERSHIP

Perhaps the most intangible, yet powerful advantage is the pride of ownership. A home gives you and your family a feeling of stability and commitment. A special sense of security and satisfaction come as you begin to put down roots in a neighborhood. Your family will enjoy the benefits of this decision for many years.

WHERE TO BEGIN

The process of buying a home can seem long and complicated—so many new words to learn and understand—deciding what you really want in a home—wondering if you can afford such a major purchase.

The first step in the purchase of a new home is to evaluate your financial status. Start by filling out this FINANCIAL OUTLINE.

FINANCIAL OUTLINE
OUR ANNUAL INCOME

Total Salaries	$ _____
Bonuses	_____
Interest Income	_____
Dividends	_____
Other	_____
TOTAL	_____

OUR MONTHLY PAYMENTS

Real Estate Loans _____

Auto Loans _____

Alimony/Child Support _____

Credit Cards:

- _____ _____

_____ _____

Insurance Premiums _____

Taxes:

Federal _____

State _____

Other Debts:

_____ _____

_____ _____

TOTAL _____

OUR ASSETS

Cash on Hand _____

Checking _____

Savings _____

Life Insurance Cash Value _____

Real Estate Owned (Market Value) _____

Vested Interest in Retirement Fund _____

Stocks, Bonds, Securities _____

Automobiles (Market Value) _____

Other: _____ _____

_____ _____

TOTAL _____

OUR LIABILITIES

Unpaid Balance

Real Estate Loans _____

Auto Loans _____

Credit Cards:

_____ _____

_____ _____

Taxes:

Federal _____

State _____

Other Debts:

_____ _____

_____ _____

TOTAL _____

5

THE DOWN PAYMENT

WHAT CAN YOU AFFORD TO SPEND ON A HOME?

The best approach in buying a home is to first understand how a home is financed. There are three crucial elements: (1) a down payment, (2) closing costs, and (3) the mortgage. When you know the amount of down payment and closing costs you can afford, and how much mortgage money you will be able to borrow, you know how much home you can buy.

DO I HAVE A DOWN PAYMENT?

A down payment is the money you pay up front toward the house. The more cash you pay as a down payment, the less you will have to pay each month on the mortgage, and the lower the interest costs will be over the life of the mortgage. Typically, a conventional lender will require 20 to 25 percent of the purchase price as a down payment.

In some cases, involving an excellent credit history and sufficient income, lenders will agree to a 10 percent down payment. This may give you more cash for other moving expenses, but it will also increase your monthly mortgage payments.

Loans through the Federal Housing Administration (FHA) or Veterans Administration (VA) carry very attractive down payment requirements of five percent or less. There is usually a maximum on the amount of money you can borrow with these types of loans, and VA loans are only available to veterans. FHA and VA loans are available at competitive interest rates. An additional benefit is that the seller may pay part of the points. In addition, when the time comes to sell, the next buyer may be able to assume the loan, subject to certain conditions.

If permissible, secondary financing may be used as an alternative way to finance your new home. This means that the seller may hold a second mortgage for 10 percent of the purchase price, while the buyer puts 10 percent cash down.

6

CLOSING COSTS

Typically, conventional lenders are willing to accept a lower down payment if private mortgage insurance (PMI) is secured. PMI protects the lender in case of default on the loan. It will cost more, but it can reduce your down payment to 10 percent.

WHAT ARE CLOSING COSTS?

Closing costs are simply this: the costs of borrowing money, establishing the loan, and preparing the necessary documents to finalize the sale. These costs may be significant and are easily overlooked by a first-time buyer:

(1) The Costs of Borrowing Money. This includes what some lenders call "discount points," a one-time charge to adjust the yield on the loan to what market conditions demand. Each point equals one percent of the mortgage amount. Two and one-half points on a $100,000 mortgage would cost $2,500.

(2) The Costs of Establishing a Loan. These might include the loan origination fee, appraisal fee, and cost of credit reports. Premiums for hazard and mortgage insurance are usually paid at closing. Also, prepaid interest will be collected for the period between closing and the end of the purchase month.

(3) The Costs of Document Preparation. Title costs pay for the search of public records to determine if the property you want to purchase is free from any other ownership or liens. Recording and transfer fees cover the legal recording of the deed with the proper governmental agencies as well as the transfer of taxes.

Overall closing costs vary from state to state. Check with your CENTURY 21® office for an estimate of your closing costs.

HOW DO I FINANCE MY HOME?

The single most important aspect of your home purchase is the loan, or mortgage, you obtain. The amount of this loan will be decided by the price of the home and your down payment.

Generally, the amount of your down payment and income/debts control the price range of homes you can look for, and hence, the size of loan you will need.

A lender will analyze your income to determine your ability to repay the loan. A general rule of thumb to calculate how much loan payment you can handle is to figure 25-33 percent of your gross, pre-tax monthly income.

The interest rate and the principal amount of the mortgage will determine the amount of your monthly payments. The higher the interest rate, the higher the monthly payments. The length of most real estate loans is generally 15 or 30 years.

The following Monthly Payments Chart will help you figure the maximum payment you can afford. Note that you must also add property taxes, home insurance costs, and homeowner's association fees, if any, to these figures for a complete, realistic monthly obligation.

operty Address: _____

$ _____
Purchase price

TIMATED EXPENSES:

gination Fee - 1% ....
nts (Buyer or seller can pay) ....
n Fee ....
Fun ing Fee - 1% (can be financed) ....
y if less than 20% down) ....
% (can be financed) ....
- (one month) ....
Fee ....
nent Fee ....
ssing Fee ....
A Title Policy - (loan amount) ....
Service - $60 ....
mpounds/ProRations (six months) ....
ance Policy (hazard fire, HO) ....
it Report - $50 ....
Assoc. Dues/Land Lease Fee ....
aisal Fee ....
l Insurance ....
e Warranty - (optional) ....
(Notary, Recording, Other) ....

proximate Total Costs ....
wn Payment ....
al Cash Required ....
Monthly Payment ....

MONTHLY PAYMENTS

MONTHLY PAYMENTS CHART
BASED ON A 30-YEAR FIXED-RATE MORTGAGE

LOAN AMOUNT	INTEREST RATE								
	8%	8.5%	9.0%	9.5%	10.0%	10.5%	11.0%	11.5%	12.0%
$40,000	$293	$308	$322	$336	$351	$366	$381	$396	$411
$45,000	$330	$346	$362	$378	$395	$412	$429	$446	$463
$50,000	$367	$384	$402	$420	$439	$457	$476	$495	$514
$55,000	$404	$423	$443	$462	$483	$503	$524	$545	$566
$60,000	$440	$461	$483	$505	$527	$549	$571	$594	$617
$65,000	$477	$500	$523	$547	$570	$595	$619	$644	$669
$70,000	$514	$538	$563	$589	$614	$640	$667	$693	$720
$75,000	$550	$577	$603	$631	$658	$686	$714	$743	$771
$80,000	$587	$615	$644	$673	$702	$732	$762	$792	$823
$85,000	$624	$654	$684	$715	$746	$778	$809	$842	$874
$90,000	$660	$692	$724	$757	$790	$823	$857	$891	$926
$95,000	$697	$730	$764	$799	$834	$869	$905	$941	$977
$100,000	$734	$769	$805	$841	$878	$915	$952	$990	$1,029
$105,000	$770	$807	$845	$883	$921	$960	$1,000	$1,040	$1,080
$110,000	$807	$846	$885	$925	$965	$1,006	$1,048	$1,089	$1,131
$115,000	$844	$884	$925	$967	$1,009	$1,052	$1,096	$1,139	$1,183
$120,000	$881	$923	$966	$1,009	$1,053	$1,098	$1,143	$1,188	$1,234

Find your approximate loan amount, read across to your applicable interest rate—this is your approximate monthly payment, amortized.

NOTE: You must also add property taxes, home insurance costs, and home-owner's association fees, if any, to these figures for a complete, realistic monthly obligation.

Loans fall into two basic categories: *(1) those that have fixed interest rates and payments; and (2) those with interest rates and payments that vary over time.*

A fixed rate mortgage provides a known monthly payment that will remain the same throughout the life of the loan. This means housing costs will never vary and will be easy to budget. The interest rates on these loans are usually a little higher than adjustable loans since the lender is establishing a set interest for many years.

MORTGAGES

Adjustable Rate Mortgage (ARM) loans generally give you the benefit of low initial interest rates and a corresponding lower monthly payment at the beginning of the loan term. The rates increase (or may even decrease) as the loan provides for periodic changes in interest rates. An important point to look for is the presence or absence of interest-rate "caps." Life-of-the-loan caps place a ceiling on how high the rate can go over the term of the loan, often five to six percentage points above the original rate. They are a guarantee from the lender that you will not be required to pay more than the agreed-upon maximum interest rate. Annual caps protect you from extreme jumps in the interest rate in any given year and are usually in the one to two percent range.

Shop around for your loan. Don't be afraid to ask questions and to compare one loan to another. Since you will be living with it for many years, make sure to get the one best suited to your financial circumstances. For more information, consult the CENTURY 21® Home Finance Guide.

WHAT TO LOOK FOR IN A HOME

The best way to prepare for the home search is to be clear about your needs and wants before you look. Buying a home can be an emotional experience.

First of all, decide where you want to live. Location is the single most important factor in buying a new home. It will partially determine the price of the home and will be a powerful influence on your lifestyle.

If you are from out-of-town, ask co-workers and acquaintances for their recommendations. Rely on the services of a real estate professional. They make it their business to know the area—with its neighborhoods, shopping and schools.

YOUR SEARCH

Once you've identified a general geographic area for your new residence, decide what you want in a home. There are two basic choices, *(1) a new or an existing structure, and (2) a single family home or a condominium/co-op.*

The "new" versus "existing" question means weighing the benefits of established neighborhoods and sometimes superior building materials against the latest in amenities, appliances and style. Purchasing a new home requires the added expenses of window coverings, upgrades in carpeting, landscaping, and a great deal of time and patience. To many, an existing home that has been well cared for is much more attractive than a new home requiring months of decision making and cash outlay.

A single family home gives you the most privacy and choice. It is generally more spacious than a condo and provides yard space for children to play and outdoor hobbies such as gardening. Landscaping can be designed to be maintenance-free, giving maximum enjoyment for minimum work. Condos and co-ops free you from the burden of general upkeep and provide common areas with pools and other recreational facilities. They are also usually more affordable.

Narrowing your search to homes with specific features will save you lots of time. Take a look at our "Want List" on page 12. Use this list, or create your own, to define your future home. Of course, your final selection may require compromise on some of these points.

PRIORITIES

WANT LIST

	PRIORITY		
	High	Medium	Low

TYPE OF HOME

	High	Medium	Low
Existing Structure	___	___	___
New Construction	___	___	___
Single Family, detached	___	___	___
Condominium/Townhouse	___	___	___

LOCATION

	High	Medium	Low
Commute Time	___	___	___
Less than 15 mins.	___	___	___
Less than 30 mins.	___	___	___
Less than 45 mins.	___	___	___
Neighborhood	___	___	___
Part of an Association	___	___	___
Parks	___	___	___
Pools	___	___	___
Bike Paths	___	___	___
Nearby Shopping	___	___	___
_____	___	___	___
_____	___	___	___
_____	___	___	___
School District	___	___	___
Particular district	___	___	___
Schools within walking distance	___	___	___
Near Public Transportation	___	___	___

FEATURES

	High	Medium	Low
Particular Architectural Style	___	___	___
_____	___	___	___
Levels	___	___	___
1 story	___	___	___
2 story	___	___	___
Split	___	___	___
Number of Bedrooms: _____	___	___	___
Number of Bathrooms: _____	___	___	___
Large Yard	___	___	___
Basement	___	___	___
Garage (_____ -Car)	___	___	___
Eat-in-kitchen	___	___	___
Separate Dining Room	___	___	___
Family Room	___	___	___
Fireplace	___	___	___
Central Heat	___	___	___
Central Air	___	___	___
Pool	___	___	___
_____	___	___	___
_____	___	___	___
_____	___	___	___
_____	___	___	___

PROFESSIONAL HELP

A REAL ESTATE SALES ASSOCIATE CAN HELP

Searching for your dream house is no easy job. A real estate sales associate's knowledge, experience and access to the properties can simplify the process. A sales associate who participates in the Multiple Listing Service (MLS) has access to many homes for sale.

After learning of your specific housing needs, a professional sales associate can screen the homes, finding those most suitable to show you. This can save you time, money and effort. Your sales associate can also supply information on home values, taxes, utility costs, neighborhoods, and financing.

Selecting the right real estate company is an important decision. The CENTURY 21® system is the world's largest real estate sales organization with over 7000 offices in the United States, Canada, Japan, France, the United Kingdom and Australia. Each CENTURY 21 office is independently owned and operated, and is staffed by local sales professionals who are trained to assist you with your home purchase.

Now that you've read through this booklet, give us a call. Let us help you and your family find just the right home.

GLOSSARY

GLOSSARY OF REAL ESTATE TERMS

ARM — Adjustable Rate Mortgage — A loan that allows the interest rate to be changed periodically.

Agency — A legal relationship in which an owner-principal engages a broker-agent in the sale of property or buyer-principal engages a broker-agent in the purchase of property.

APR — Annual Percentage Rate — The total finance charge (interest, loan fees, points) expressed as a percentage of the loan amount.

Amortization — The gradual repayment of a mortgage by periodic installments.

Appraisal — An estimate of the value of a property.

Assessed Value — The valuation placed on property by a public tax assessor as the basis of property taxes.

Assumption of Mortgage — Agreement by the buyer to assume responsibility for a mortgage owned by the seller; the seller remains liable to the lender unless the lender agrees to release him.

Balloon Mortgage — A mortgage that has a substantial amount of the principal due at the maturity of the note.

Broker — A person licensed by a state real estate commission to act independently in conducting a real estate brokerage business. Although the requirements for a broker's license vary from state to state, an individual usually must have one or more years of experience in the industry and pass an examination.

Buydowns — When a home buyer, or a third party, puts up an amount of money sufficient to "buy" or obtain a lower-than-market interest rate from a lending institution.

Cap — A maximum amount of interest that can be charged.

Closing — The final step in transferring ownership of a property from seller to buyer.

Closing Costs — Fees and expenses, not including the price of the home, payable by the seller and the buyer at the time of closing (e.g., brokerage commissions, title insurance premiums, inspection and appraisal fees.)

Condominium — Ownership which involves a separation of property into individual ownership elements and common ownership elements.

Contingency — A condition that must be satisfied before a contract is binding.

Conventional Loan — A fixed-rate, fixed-term loan that is made without government insurance.

Co-op — A buyer purchases shares in a co-op corporation, made up of the residents in the co-op property. The buyer owns the shares rather than owning the real property. In exchange, the buyer has the right to occupy a co-op unit.

Deed — A legal document conveying title to a property.

Earnest Money — A payment given to the seller by a potential buyer indicating the buyer's intent to complete the purchase of the property.

Equity — The owner's value or interest in a property.

Escrow — The placement of money or documents with a third party for safekeeping pending the fulfillment or performance of a specific act or condition.

FHA Mortgage — A mortgage loan insured by the Federal Housing Administration, permitting lenders to offer better terms.

Fixed-rate Mortgage — A loan that has only one stated interest rate.

HUD — Housing and Urban Development — A U.S. governmental agency established to implement certain federal housing and community development programs.

Lien — A legal claim against a property that must be paid when property is sold.

Loan Origination Fee — The charge you must pay to the lender for processing your mortgage.

Market value — The highest price a ready, willing and able buyer will pay and the lowest price a seller will accept.

Mortgage — A lien on real estate given by the buyer as security for money borrowed from a lender.

Mortgage Insurance — A policy that provides protection for the lender in case of default and guarantees repayment of the loan in the event of the death or disability of the borrower.

MLS — Multiple Listing Service

Points — A dollar amount, expressed as a percentage of the mortgage amount, which is paid to a lender as a consideration for making a loan. A point is 1% of the amount of the mortgage loan; also called discount points.

P&I — Principal and Interest Payment — A periodic (usually monthly) payment that includes the interest charges for the period plus an amount applied to amortization of the principal balance.

PITI — Principal, Interest, Taxes, and Insurance Payment — The periodic payment that includes a principal and interest payment plus a contribution to the escrow account set up by the lender to pay insurance premiums and property taxes on the mortgage property.

REALTOR® and REALTOR ASSOCIATE — Registered collective membership marks that identify real estate professionals who are members of the National Association of REALTORS and subscribe to its strict Code of Ethics.

Title — A document that is evidence of ownership.

Title Insurance — Protection for lenders and homeowners against financial loss resulting from legal defects in the title.

Title Search — A check of title records to identify liens, encumbrances and ownership rights to the property.

VA Mortgage — A mortgage loan guaranteed by the Veterans Administration, an agency of the federal government that provides services for eligible veterans.

Printed in U.S.A. by
Smith Lithographic Arts
Form No. 1-4050

Equal Housing Opportunity

Each Office is Independently Owned and Operated